# WREATHS

FRESH FORAGED FOLIAGE

# WREATHS

FRESH
FORAGED
FOLIAGE
&
FAUX

Alys Dobbie

SCHIFFER
PUBLISHING
4880 Lower Valley Road • Atglen, PA 19310

Other Schiffer Books on Related Subjects:

*Floral Accessories,* Wendy Andrade, ISBN 978-0-7643-5446-5

*Fresh Floral Jewelry: Creating Wearable Art with Wendy Andrade, NDSF, AIFD, FBFA,* Wendy Andrade, ISBN 978-0-7643-4411-4

*Entertaining with Flowers: The Floral Artistry of Bill Murphy,* Bill Murphy, ISBN 978-0-7643-2556-4

© 2021 Design and layout BlueRed Press
© 2021 Text and images Alys Dobbie
Photography by Ian Copestake

Library of Congress Control Number: 2020952447

All rights reserved. No part of this work may be reproduced or used in any form or by any means—graphic, electronic, or mechanical, including photocopying or information storage and retrieval systems—without written permission from the publisher.

The scanning, uploading, and distribution of this book or any part thereof via the internet or any other means without the permission of the publisher is illegal and punishable by law. Please purchase only authorized editions and do not participate in or encourage the electronic piracy of copyrighted materials.

"Schiffer," "Schiffer Publishing, Ltd.," and the pen and inkwell logo are registered trademarks of Schiffer Publishing, Ltd.

Produced by BlueRed Press Ltd. 2021
Designed by Insight Design Concepts Ltd.
Type set in Montserrat

ISBN: 978-0-7643-6212-5
Printed in India

Published by Schiffer Publishing, Ltd.
4880 Lower Valley Road
Atglen, PA 19310
Phone: (610) 593-1777; Fax: (610) 593-2002
Email: *Info@schifferbooks.com*
Web: *www.schifferbooks.com*

For our complete selection of fine books on this and related subjects, please visit our website at www.schifferbooks.com. You may also write for a free catalog.

Schiffer Publishing's titles are available at special discounts for bulk purchases for sales promotions or premiums. Special editions, including personalized covers, corporate imprints, and excerpts, can be created in large quantities for special needs. For more information, contact the publisher.

We are always looking for people to write books on new and related subjects. If you have an idea for a book, please contact us at *proposals@schifferbooks.com.*

This book is dedicated to Victoria, who was tireless in her assistance in putting this book together.

# Contents

## INTRODUCTION — 6
Tools — 8
Techniques — 11
Cheats — 12
Maintenance — 13

## LIVING WREATHS — 14
Succulent Wreath — 16
Herb Garden Wreath — 22
Mixed Live Moss Wreath — 28
Fresh Flower Wreath — 32
Spring Bulb Wreath — 40

## DRIED WREATHS — 46
Dried Flowers and Foliage Wreath — 48
Paper Flower Wreath — 54
Feather Wreath — 66
Pine Cone Wreath — 72
Rag Wreath — 80

## OCCASION WREATHS — 86
Christmas Bauble Wreath — 88
Pop-Pom Wreath — 94
Felt Flower Wreath — 100
Easter Egg Wreath — 112
Halloween Wreath — 118

## TEMPLATES — 126

# INTRODUCTION

Upon hearing the word "wreaths," people automatically assume that we're talking about the "C" word—Christmas. In reality, front doors look gorgeous adorned with wreaths all year around. So here is a selection of exciting, elegant, and artistic wreaths for seasonal celebrations across the full twelve months of the year. This book can provide you with more than one option for each season—and they don't just have to hang on your front door: use them inside, on the back door, and even to liven up a garden seating area. These designs really are versatile as well as attractive, and can hang anywhere!

Everyone agrees that once the Christmas tree comes down and the festive decorations are stored away, the house looks really empty. People start clamoring for large indoor houseplants to fill that green void. The same should apply to your front door—it should never be bare. Instead, make it a feature and switch up your style with the changing seasons.

For spring, why not try the fresh bulb or Easter egg wreath? Summer could host an amazing feather or dried-flower assembly or simply a selection of fresh flowers. Why not make a spooky crescent-shaped Halloween wreath for fall, and later go over the top with our extravagant bauble wreath for December?

This book gives you comprehensive instructions on the tools to buy, the materials to get, and how to source them, and then some handy techniques and tips on maintaining your beautiful wreath. Additionally, there are step-by-step guides of how to put the wreaths together.

INTRODUCTION
# Tools

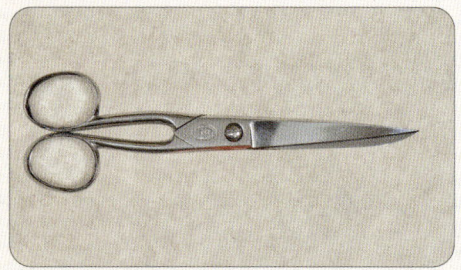 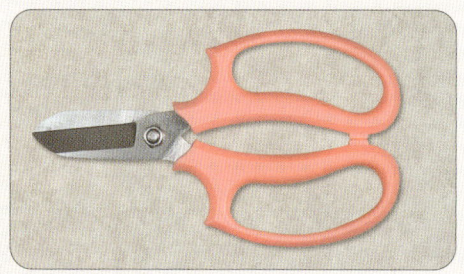 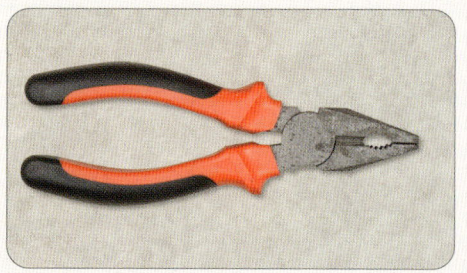

**Fabric scissors**—every tailor will tell you to keep your fabric scissors exclusively for use on fabric! Once they are used on other items, they blunt very quickly. Use these for cutting any ribbon or the material for the rag wreath.

**Floristry scissors**—designed to be hard-wearing, these scissors will cut through anything from wire to tough woody stems. If you like the look of the pink ones in this book, then search for "Japanese floristry scissors" online and you'll find some in each price bracket.

**Pliers**—great for bending or cutting metal without blunting your scissors.

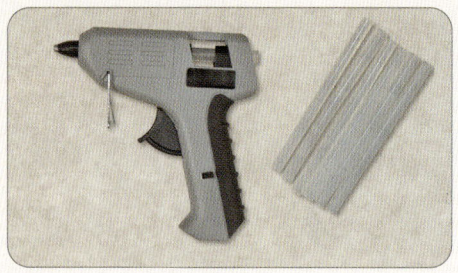  

**Glue gun**—these can be picked up in any craft store or online for a few dollars. Don't get a fancy one if you're just starting out; basic glue guns are still fine. It's handy to have a stand to catch any rogue drips, or even an old tray underneath to catch falling glue.

**Gloves**—for your own protection. Most people don't tend to use them, but if you have sensitive skin or allergies, it's a good idea to wear them, especially when handling fresh materials and spring flowering bulbs.

**Pom-pom maker**—small plastic circles or half-moons that clip together. These are available online or in craft stores, although my mother used to use just an old piece of card and wrap the wool around that—there are plenty of tutorials online!

WREATHS

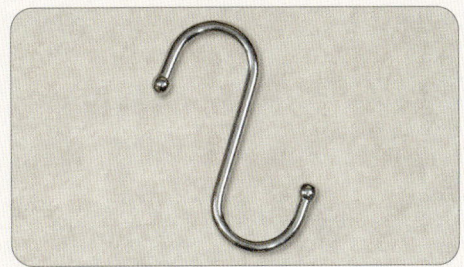  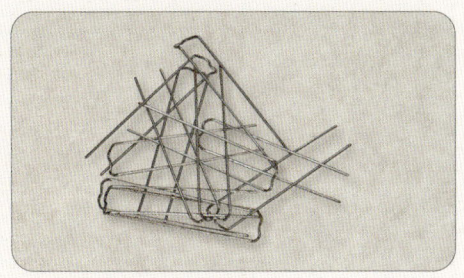

**S-hooks**—traditionally used to hang up meat or cooking equipment. I find these hooks are the easiest way to create a quick, durable hanger for door wreaths.

**Twine**—a great item to have, and so versatile: you can use it to bind things to the wreath, make the wreath bases, and make loopholes for wreaths to be hung. Endless possibilities!

**Mossing pins**—the florist's secret weapon! These bent pins are great for anchoring or attaching things to your wreaths. They are very like large, old-fashioned hairpins.

**Floristry wire**

- Binding wire is available on a reel and can be bought online or at your local floristry wholesaler. An alternative is fishing wire, but this doesn't hold in place as well.

- Green wire comes in different lengths and gauges (thicknesses). I generally go for a 22 gauge—strong enough to hold things in place, but also with some flex in it so you don't mangle your fingers when using it!

- Silver buttoning wire—this is generally a very thin wire that comes pre-cut. It is ideal for binding fussy bits on light materials.

**Mister**—just an ordinary spray bottle (even a cleaned-out detergent bottle), it's necessary for the maintenance of the fresh wreaths.

INTRODUCTION

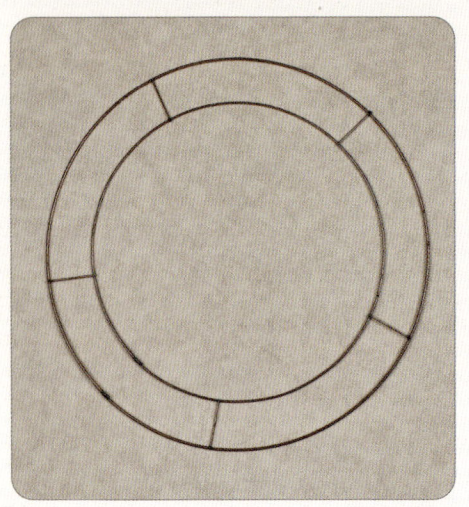

**Wreath bases**—I use four different base types in this book, but if you don't have the relevant type, don't worry—the wreaths are adaptable.

You can make straw and wicker wreaths from store-bought ingredients or forage foliage from your back yard to form into a wreath. Copper-wire bases are really cheap to buy, so I would recommend getting these, since you can always build them up to bulk them out. Polystyrene wreaths/circles aren't particularly good for the environment—hence appearing only a couple of times in the book—but they are readily available in craft stores and online if you can't get anything else.

## Templates

Template outlines are provided at the back of this book for use in two of the wreaths. You can either trace them or scan them to copy them onto card. The benefit of scanning is that the template pieces can easily be scaled up or down in size should you want to do so, as well as being easy to print off in whatever quantity you require.

# Techniques

A huge amount of floristry revolves around line, form, color, space, and texture—our featured projects can all be adapted to suit any style or materials that you have, or find in and around your home or elsewhere.

Handy techniques—what the average pupil learns at floristry school—can be acquired by watching online videos or reading a book. It's worth doing this because they will help you to no end. Some of the most useful techniques involve how to bend wire, specifically around buttonholes and other fussy bits. This will be particularly helpful when it comes to the dried wreath, as well as the fresh and feather wreaths.

**Conditioning**—this applies to fresh flowers and foliage. Start by removing the majority of excess leaves and any damaged petals or foliage. To maximize the water uptake of the stem, use a sharp pair of pruning shears and cut the stem at a 45-degree angle to the desired length.

**Gluing**—you can attach any material to any other material with the use of an appropriate adhesive. PVA, hot glue, or super glue are all good for these wreath projects. One tip when using a hot-glue gun to apply a blob of glue, is to allow the glue gun to fully heat up, then squeeze the trigger and, as you lift off, give the gun a circular spin as you stop pushing the trigger—this avoids any long, sticky, glue gun trails!

**Pinning**—a mossing pin works for any material (soft or hard) that needs to be attached to another material. Simply push the pin directly through the material, ensuring it makes good contact with the surface of the material it is being attached to.

**Tying**—simple means of securing one material to another by tying a knot or a bow.

**Weaving**—typically a long length of material is used to decorate or secure another material to itself, by threading it in and out of another material (almost like sewing). Weaving is both decorative and functional.

**Wiring**—using a length of wire to secure one material to another, usually by wrapping and bending. Wires come in many different gauges or strengths. As a general rule, the object you are wiring should be supported by the chosen wire without bending. Buy floristry wire or reel wire for these projects.

**Pom-poms**
If you don't have a pom-pom maker, you can make your own.

1. Cut two circles of strong card to the desired size of your pom-pom.

2. Cut a small section into the center of both circles to make a C-shape.

3. Wrap the yarn around the card circles, starting at one end, until you have wrapped all of the card. (It should end up looking like a wool donut.)

4. Using sharp scissors, cut in between the yarn on the outside edge, using the outer edge of the card as a guide.

5. Once fully cut, gently pull apart the card circles. Using a small length of wool or strong thread, tie a few tight knots to secure the pom-pom.

Now remove the card and fluff, trim, and shape your finished pom-pom!

INTRODUCTION

- Read up on floristry tips and techniques. There are plenty of free online resources to get you started. Pinterest is also a great place to look for inspiration, especially if you want a particular color theme or style. Other sources of inspiration can come from anywhere—magazines, social media, books—anything that inspires you to create!

- If you don't have mossing pins, simply cut short lengths of sturdy wire and bend them in half to create a pin (like an old-fashioned U-shaped hairpin).

- If you don't own a glue gun or prefer not to use one, most of the projects in this book will work just as well with super glue or a strong adhesive. It'll just take a little while longer to dry, so don't move the wreath or hang it up too soon!

- If you don't have any S-hooks, you can use various other methods to hang your finished wreaths. Try using strong ribbon or twine wrapped around the top of the wreath to make a hanging loop. This can be simple and discreet, or you can make it into a statement. You can also simply hang your wreath directly from a hook or a nail—especially if your wreath has a wire frame. Just make sure you choose a suitably strong attachment to hold the wreath up, since they can get quite heavy!

- To make the perfect bow: take a length of twine or ribbon and fold the length in half. Using the fingers on both hands, create an M-shape. Now wrap and tuck one of the loops of the M around the other, and loosen or tighten accordingly. You can trim the excess off the tails or leave them trailing.

- Drying your own flowers or foliage is easy: choose hardy plant material (avoid anything soft-stemmed such as sunflowers, tulips, or lilies, since these do not dry as well and can go moldy). Simply take a bundle and tie them up at the base with twine (or string) and hang them upside down in a cool and dry place: this process can take a while, but it's worth it! The flowers and foliage that work best are eucalyptus, roses, gyposophia, hydrangeas, and lavender; twigs are a great and free addition.

# Maintenance

**Glue gun**—your best friend. With wreaths that consist of man-made materials (and even those made of feathers or dried flowers, come to think of it!), a glue gun is going to help you out of any situation. Expect things to fall off as you are making it. Also, since your wreath is likely to be hung on your door, expect it to be knocked about a fair amount, so make it as robust as possible.

**Dust, dust, dust**—wreaths can age really quickly by gathering dust. Make sure you take your wreaths down and give them a good clean every now and again. Also, try to keep any of the wreaths that have man-made materials out of direct sun and well away from any open flames such as candles! The sun will make bright colors fade, and a lot of these materials are flammable.

**Misting bottle**—with any of the fresh wreaths using bulbs, moss, spring flowers, succulents, or herbs, a misting bottle is going to be really helpful. Not only will it prolong the life of all these fresh wreaths, it's going to make the items look fresher and greener for longer. However, note that for the succulent wreath, mist only the moss, not the succulents—they hate humidity!

**Mossing pins**—these will secure almost anything in place. They are traditionally used in floristry to hold everything together, but these guys will be helpful for a quick fix for pretty much anything that might fall off—they literally pin things into place

**Sink**—you'll notice that all fresh wreaths dry out incredibly quickly. The best way to inject moisture into them is to take them down (the moss based ones only) and place them in a bath or sink that has about an inch of tepid water in it. Leave it in there for about ten minutes and then let the water out of the sink and place the wreath on the drainboard for a few hours to let the excess water run off. The moss should have soaked up the water, and you'll be good to go for a few more weeks.

**Watering**—most of the planted wreaths would actually benefit from being kept flat for the first few weeks of their lives to establish themselves. I would recommend watering the wreath as above, and then leaving it for about two weeks, then perhaps repeating the watering before hanging up. Be careful, because these live wreaths can become very heavy, especially when well watered.

# Living Wreaths

# Succulent Wreath

This living wreath is truly unique because it will completely change over time! As the plants grow, the wreath will fill out. You can use any low-growing succulents such as echeverias or aloes, and you can also use cuttings from your established succulents. The moist moss will help them all flourish quickly. Grouping the succulents by color is also a fun way to display them—it gives almost an ombré rainbow effect. This wreath can be hung indoors or outside.

### Tools
Gloves (optional)
Large tweezers
Mister
Scissors

### Materials
Binding wire
Copper wreath ring
Miniature succulent selection, about 28—30 plants
Sphagnum moss
S-hook

LIVING WREATHS

1

2a

2b

3a

3b

4

# WREATHS

1. Divide the sphagnum moss up into tennis-ball-sized shapes. Place one on top of the copper wreath ring, and unravel some of the binding wire. Start wrapping the wire around the moss to hold it in place.

2. Carry on attaching the moss to the copper ring in the same manner. Don't pull the binding wire too tight, though, since it will make the surface area of the moss too small.

3. When you get back around to the beginning, chop the wire and poke the end into the moss to hide it.

4. Place the succulents around your wreath, and arrange them carefully, balancing their different textures, shapes, and colors. The key is to make sure that no two of the same variety are next to each other (unless, that is, you are deliberately clustering them for effect).

5. When you've decided on your scheme, remove the succulents from their pots by gently squeezing each pot. Carefully tease away as much dirt from the roots as you can.

6. With your forefinger or thumb, create a small hole that is as deep as the moss is to the ring.

7. The hole should not be wider in diameter than your finger width. You can use a small stick or large tweezers if you find it helps.

LIVING WREATHS

8. Choose your first plant and place the roots in the hole you have just made. Try to tuck in all the roots, but don't worry if some stray a bit.

9. You can secure the succulent base with mossing pins. If you still feel that your succulents are too loose, then you can straddle a couple of the leaves with these mossing pins.

10. Carry on with this method until you have placed most of your succulents on your wreath.

In between finishing this wreath and hanging it up, the wreath must have a period of up to three weeks' rest. This is to let the succulents root themselves properly—it also makes it easier to water them later. If you are too impatient for this, you can hang it up, but you almost certainly will need more mossing pins to hold the succulents in place to begin with, and you must frequently bring it down to water the plants.

Watering can be done in two ways: you can constantly spritz the back of the wreath while it's hanging (little and often). Or, if you have a bath or a wide sink, you can bring the whole thing down and submerge it in about half an inch of water (but be careful not to get the leaves of the succulents wet). Leave the wreath submerged for about ten minutes; after this, let the water drain away and place it on a drainboard for a few hours to get rid of any excess water.

You can spruce up your succulent wreath by using dangly succulents such as string of beads or *Rhipsalis* (mistletoe cacti) as shown on the page opposite. They can be pinned onto the moss by their fronds, or you can plant them as the other ones have been planted.

**Tip:**
Mix and match your plant selection to suit your style—you can use cacti if you'd like this wreath to sit flat on a table, but don't drench it with water!

# Herb Garden Wreath

Is there anything better than an edible wreath? I mean, I know this isn't made of chocolate, but a living herb wreath?! Fabulous! This wreath is very versatile since it can live on a table or on a door. It just requires really regular misting and watering. Put whatever herbs you like on this—you could even sow some edible flower seeds for a splash of color and see if they pop through. Also, the more you pinch the herbs out, the bushier they'll get.

## Tools
Gloves (optional)
Mister
Trowel

## Materials
Copper wreath ring
Flat moss
Mixed potted herbs
Mossing pins
Reel wire
S-hook
Soil

LIVING WREATHS

WREATHS

1. Water the herb plants well before you start the wreath, ideally the day before. You want them to have a good drink before planting them up.

   To start, lay out the flat moss—the image in the photo is with the moss face up, but you need to work on it face down initially.

2. With your trowel, make a ring of dirt on the moss base.

3. Place the copper ring on the dirt.

4. Cover the copper base with more dirt.

5. Unpot the herbs and remove as much dirt as possible around the roots without damaging them.

6. Make a hole in the middle of the wreath—try not to remove the moss, but tear it so that there is some in excess.

7. Your herbs should be ready to plant. Place your first one on the wreath ring and gently pull the moss over the root system (the roots should be covered and the moss should be revealed). This takes at least two hands!

8. When the moss has been successfully molded around the root base, use your reel wire to fix it in place. Holding down the wire with a spare thumb, wrap it under and around the entire wreath ring and over the moss and root system to hold everything in place. Do not cut the wire until you have worked your way around to the start again.

LIVING WREATHS

9.  The first one is the hardest, I promise! Now put your next herb into place and carry on the reel wire around the wreath ring, going under the moss and over the moss where it is pinched up around the base of the herb roots.

10. Plant the remainder of your herbs.

11. When the last one is in, wrap the binding wire a few times around the wreath ring to secure all the plants. Cut the wire and poke it into the wreath.

Your wreath will probably need to establish itself before hanging—I suggest using it as a center piece for a table while the roots grow. Keep the wreath flat for a month. Water every week—potentially more in the summer months—and mist it frequently. Also, remove dead leaves regularly to encourage new growth. After three or four weeks, carefully hang it up.

**Tip:**
Mix and match your herb selection to meet your personal tastes—or plant just one of your favorites for maximum impact. Avoid growing tall herbs like fennel and dill.

# Mixed Live Moss Wreath

This moss wreath is really for nature lovers and looks fab hung on rustic doors or above antique fireplaces. The reindeer moss can be a little pricey, so you can always just stick to using homegrown and natural mosses. But be warned—they take a lot more maintenance, so arm yourself with a misting bottle and you'll be away! You can always combine this with the pine cone wreath, and just add anything you find while foraging.

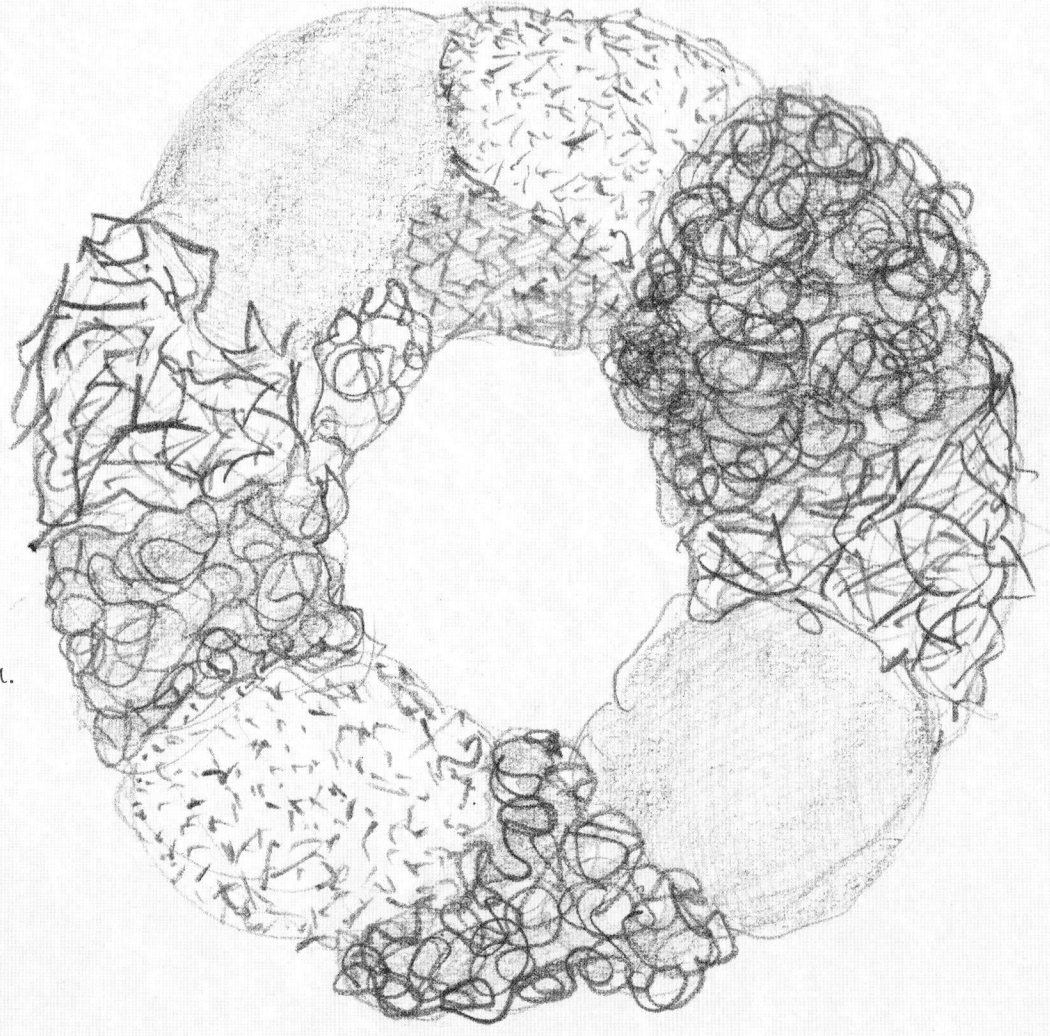

## Tools
Mister
Scissors

## Materials
Copper wreath ring, 12 in. (30 cm) diameter
Fresh bun moss
Mossing pins
Reindeer moss
Reel wire
Silver moss
Sphagnum moss

# LIVING WREATHS

Lay out all of your materials. Create a base for your wreath as per steps 1, 2, and 3 for the Succulent Wreath on page 19.

1. Make a tennis-ball-sized shape of moss, and, using a mossing pin, pin it onto the sphagnum base.

2. Carry on around the wreath, using the different mosses in turn. Use mossing pins to press each piece onto the base.

Ta-da! You can use an S-hook to hang this wreath up, or you could use it a table centerpiece. Remember to mist this wreath regularly to keep the moss looking fresh—especially in hot weather.

**Tip:**
Use what you have—moss can be expensive, so you could opt for completely faux moss, less maintenance! If collecting from the wild, take only what you need from sustainable (and legal) sources. Many florists will sell cultivated moss.

# Fresh Flower Wreath

The beauty of this wreath is that you can buy any ordinary supermarket flowers and make something spectacular. They make great alternatives to your average predictable bouquet. Fresh flowers will change from season to season—in the UK, a spring wreath would feature lots of daffodils and tulips; in the summer, some heavy garden roses. The fall could show off muted deep-orange colors (with the odd dahlia, perhaps?), and for winter, some whites, silvers, and eucalyptus would look incredible.

## Tools
Gloves (optional)
Mister
Scissors

## Materials
Binding wire
Copper wreath ring
Foliage — some of my favorites are eucalyptus and ruscus
Flowers — get seasonal flowers or pick some from your yard
Textural berried flowers
Sphagnum moss

LIVING WREATHS

1

2

3

4

5

6

WREATHS

Create a base for your wreath as per steps 1, 2, and 3 for the Succulent Wreath on page 19.

1. Put all the materials out so you can see what you have all together. Start off by conditioning the foliage. This literally means just cutting it to size and removing some of the lower leaves. Cut the foliage down to about 6–8 in. (15–20 cm) in length. Here, I'm using eucalyptus stems.

2. Once you have made your wreath base, start by poking the foliage into the outer ring of the sphagnum moss, beginning with the background base foliage and layering it up.

3. Try to fill all the gaps around the wreath with a light covering of the background foliage; otherwise you will use triple what you need to, and weigh the wreath down in the process!

4. Use two or three different types of foliage for texture. I have used two different types of eucalyptus leaves.

5. Once the outer is complete, start infilling the inner ring with short pieces of foliage around 4 in. (10 cm) long.

6. When that is complete, you should still be able to see a central ring of moss.

7. Start placing foliage around 4–6 in. (10–15 cm) long on the central ring, standing vertically (if your wreath is set on a table).

# LIVING WREATHS

8

11

9

12

10

13

WREATHS

8. Finish this off, but don't worry if some of the moss is still visible.

9. Begin conditioning your flowers. With flowers that have soft leaves and no thorns, you can hold on to the top of the stem and, with one hand, pull downward on the stem in the opposite direction of growth.

10. For flowers with tougher stalks, such as the ones pictured here—simply cut them down to size, removing all lower leaves, and thorns if necessary.

11. Again, do the same with any flowers that don't have lower foliage; simply cut down to size, about 5 in. (12 cm).

12. With roses or anything else with rough stems, cut off the abrasive bits or use a thorn remover.

13. Begin by placing the most prominent (or focal) flower in the wreath. You literally just poke the stem into the sphagnum moss. I began with the red rose.

14. Carry on around the wreath; try to place the flowers randomly and not too regularly. You don't want the wreath to look too formal.

15. Time to add the other flowers in; it's most effective to do clusters of mixed flowers or color tones, to give a rhythm to the composition.

LIVING WREATHS

16. Insert your smallest flowers last, before putting any textural berries or anything else in.

17. Put your smallest textural berries in.

Hang the wreath from an S-hook and continue to mist it with fresh water to keep it fresher for longer.

**Tip:**
Change up your color palette with the seasons or use all foliage for a fresh green alternative that can be 100 percent foraged. The wreath base can be reused time and again. Simply remove the flowers and foliage once they are past their best, and replace with new ones. At the same time, soak the moss base in water to rehydrate it.

WREATHS

# Spring Bulb Wreath

Ideally, you would make this wreath between late fall and early December, since some of the bulbs will take a few months to start sprouting. When buying bulbs, check the labels and see when is the ideal sowing time. In the UK you can buy already potted hyacinths and muscari in the spring—these are great for an instant fix and pops of color to make in February–March. Alternatively, this can be used as a table centerpiece—just make sure it's on a big plate so it doesn't mark your table!

### Tools
Gloves (optional)
Large tweezers
Scissors

### Materials
Copper wreath ring
Decorative sticks, bark, etc.
Mixed spring bulbs
Mossing pins
Reel wire
Sphagnum moss

# LIVING WREATHS

1

2

3

4

5

6

# WREATHS

7

Lay out all of your materials. Create a base for your wreath as per steps 1, 2, and 3 for the Succulent Wreath on page 19.

1. Start off by placing your largest decorative item on the wreath. You will work from this—in our case we have foraged a piece of driftwood.

2. Using the reel wire, wrap it around some of the more inconspicuous parts of the wood, hiding as much of the wire as possible. If you can't hide it, don't worry too much; it won't be that visible once it is on the door.

3. With some of the completely closed bulbs, you will need to "plant" them in the moss. To do this, simply dig out a small hole with your finger, insert the bulb, and close over.

4. Plant all the bulbs first, then you can attach other things to the wreath on top.

5. For a nice artistic wreath, also place some of the bulbs on top of the sphagnum so you can see them. Use mossing pins to anchor them in place, or even pierce the bulbs to keep them in the right spot, though you do risk damaging them if you do so.

6. Once the smaller bulbs are in, plant some of the larger bulbs. Make bigger holes for the roots (as shown here).

7. Carefully unpot the bulb you want to use, removing as much of the dirt as possible without disturbing or breaking the roots.

LIVING WREATHS

8

9

8. Plant the bulb by wedging it into the hole that you made.

9. Cement its position by using the mossing pins—you can slightly pierce the bulb or use the pins as anchors over the edges of the bulbs.

This wreath would look stunning as a table centerpiece or on a sideboard, or other suitable surface where it can be seen and admired. Be sure to place it on something like a large plate so you can just pour water directly onto that plate and let the moss soak it up. Alternatively, if you intend to hang it on a door, just give the wreath around two or three weeks sitting flat to establish, and then you can hang it up by whichever method you please.

**Tip:**
Use your favorite springtime flowering plants for a splash of color and wave of scent. For a really earthy feel, decorate the wreath with bark, twigs, and moss.

# Dried Wreaths

# Dried Flowers and Foliage Wreath

Dried flowers are exploding back onto the open market—they are so "hot" right now. Recently, due to new techniques to do with bleaching and coloring, you can, for example, make an icy-white wreath from pure ruscus or a baby-blue wreath from bunny ears. Most trend-conscious florists are selling bunches of dried flowers again. They are perfect for making your own unique, long-life, spectacular, front-door wreath—or anywhere else you want to hang one.

### Tools
Glue
Glue gun
Scissors

### Materials
Binding wire
Dried flowers
Reel wire
Ribbon
Seed pods (or try pine cones)
Straw wreath

## DRIED WREATHS

# WREATHS

1. Lay all your materials out in front of you to see what you have. Cut the dried flowers and foliage to size. You want them all to be around 8 in. (20 cm) in length.

2. Once cut down, separate all the elements into different piles. You want to begin with collecting about three pieces of different foliage, or different flower heads into little bundles. Once chosen, pick up a piece of the pre-cut, thin florists' wire.

3. Wrap the wire around the base of your miniature bouquet.

4. I recommend making all the little bundles first, before starting to attach them to the wreath base. Once accomplished, begin by laying the first one on the straw wreath and attaching it by wrapping around the reel wire. Always work in the same direction—either clockwise or counterclockwise—doesn't matter which; just be consistent. Avoid the temptation to stick all the bundles "out," since this will look messy and also they won't attach very easily.

5. Don't cut the reel wire while you continue to attach the small bundles, ensuring that the base is covered and that you are covering the inner and outer sides of the wreath. Carry on wiring in bundles until you are back where you started—once there, lift up the original bundle, and work so that you don't tie it in with your new bundle.

6. When finished, chop the wire and poke it into the wreath to hide the end. Now start adding texture to the wreath. Do this by applying hot glue to your seed pods or pine cones, and sticking them firmly onto the foliage—be careful to avoid crushing earlier arrangements.

7. Florists work in odd numbers, so do the same. When adding these textural pieces, make sure you add only three, five, or seven of any number. If you add them in even numbers, they will make the wreath look square!

DRIED WREATHS

8. Continue working around, adding pieces of interest. Don't be afraid to add lots; the more textural the better.

9. Cut a piece of pretty ribbon and tie it around the wreath—it can be tucked under the foliage or pressed over the top to make it into a feature. Our example uses a mellow green velvet ribbon that merges tonally with the wreath as a whole.

**Tip:**
Dried flowers can be expensive to source, so why not dry your own? Most hardy flowers and foliage can be dried—store them hanging upside down in bunches in a dry, cool, place for a few months. Don't let them get wet or damp. And keep well away from sources of flames like candles and fires. Also, avoid direct sunlight since this will fade the colors. Remember to dust them frequently.

# Paper Flower Wreath

"Labor of love" are words that spring to mind when creating this wreath—but fear not; once the preparation is out of the way, this is a relatively easy wreath to construct. The crepe paper is an essential part of the kit—tissue paper would work, but it's not quite as workable. These wreaths are perfect for someone who wants a joyous spring feel to adorn their front door—without the dying flowers.

### Tools
Florists' scissors
Glue gun
Glue sticks
Tailors scissors
Templates

### Materials
Crepe paper
Floristry wire
Polystyrene balls
Polystyrene wreath

DRIED WREATHS

Set out your tools and materials in front of you, having chosen a nice selection of contrasting crepe paper, plus green for the leaves.

The templates for this wreath are on page 126. When cutting out the pieces, be careful to cut the crepe paper following the "stretch" guidelines—this way you'll be able to mold the petals correctly. For instance, with the green leaves, you want the stretch to be on the width of the leaf, so you can manipulate the paper so it stretches wider. Therefore, place the template so that the lines of the crepe paper are running from tip to base.

You can do this as you go, but the process is smoother if you do the cutting first. Keep the elements of each flower together: try not to mix them up!

## Peony

*1 peony center fringe, 4 large petals, 5 medium petals, 5 small petals*

1. Cut out the peony center fringe in yellow crepe paper. Then make cuts three-quarters of the way across the width of the paper, all the way along its length—so you end up with a long fringe of yellow paper. These will become the central stamens of the peony.

2. When it has all been snipped, glue one end of the paper.

3. Place the end of one floristry wire in the glue and begin to twist the paper tightly around it.

4. Just before you get to the end, dab another spot of glue on the paper to stick it down and hold all the bits together. You now have a length of wire with a floppy tuft of yellow strands.

5. Cut out the three different sized petals with the "stretch" on the crepe paper running horizontally (side-to-side) across the petals. Pull the petals gently apart—especially in the middle, to create a bowl-shaped curve—to give a more 3D effect.

6. Apply glue to the bottom of the petal.

7. Attach the smallest petals to the center section you've just made.

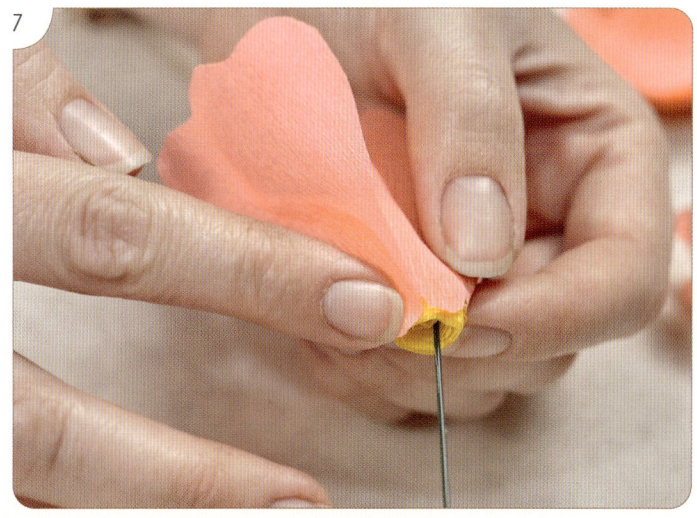

DRIED WREATHS

**Peony, continued**

8. Going up in size, attach the rest of the petals at the same point, to the smallest ones.

9. Your peony should look something like this.

10. Chop the wire down and poke it straight into the polystyrene ring.

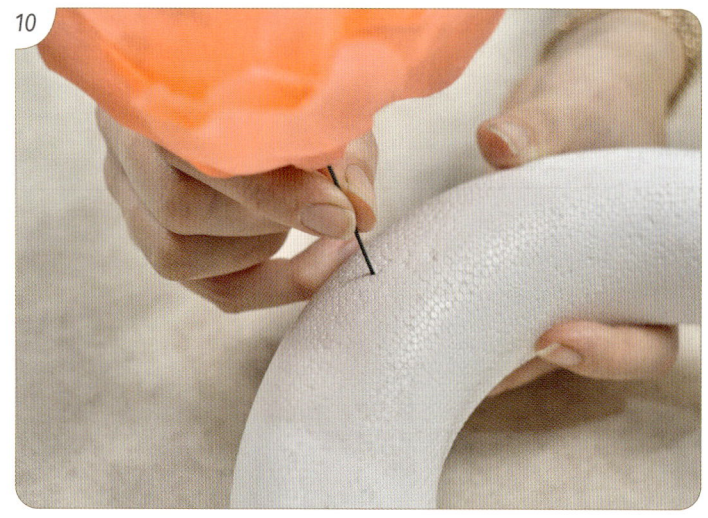

## Daisy

*1 central disc, 1 polystyrene ball, 16 daisy petals*

1. Apply hot glue to one of the small polystyrene balls.

2. Put the polystyrene ball in the center of a pre-cut circle of yellow crepe paper.

3. Wrap the paper around the ball so it sticks as neatly as possible and the ball becomes yellow.

DRIED WREATHS

# WREATHS

**Daisy, continued**

4. Put some hot glue on the other end of the polystyrene ball.

5. Close the paper around the glue, again as neatly as possible.

6. Cut the petals so that the grooves of the crepe paper are running along the longest length. Holding the petals with your forefingers and thumbs, gently pull the petals apart so they are wider than originally, and take on a 3-D effect.

7. Apply some glue to the end of the petal.

8. Glue the petal to the now-covered polystyrene ball.

9. Continue to apply the daisy petals to the covered polystyrene ball.

10. Your daisy should look something like this.

11. Glue the base of the daisy liberally.

12. Attach the daisy to the wreath.

DRIED WREATHS

1
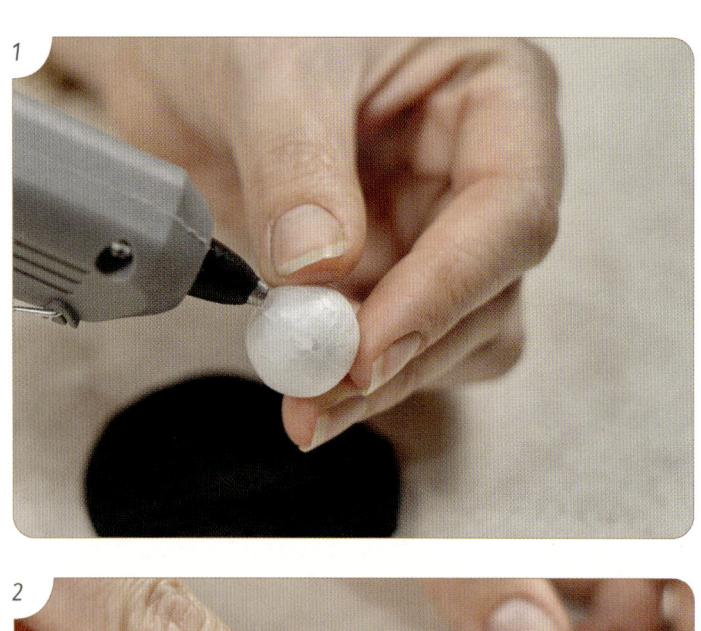

2

3

4

5
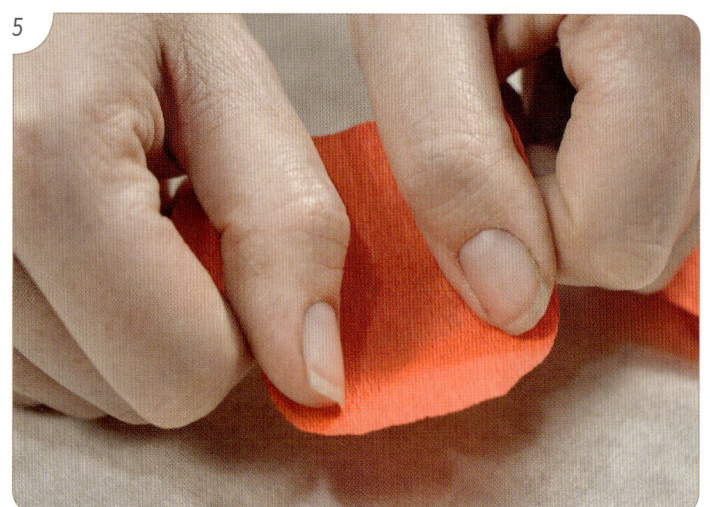

6

## Poppy

*1 central disc, 1 polystyrene ball, 8 poppy petals*

1. Apply glue to a small polystyrene ball.

2. Place the ball in the middle of your pre-cut black circle.

3. Wrap the paper around the ball as neatly as possible and apply more glue to stick the ends down.

4. Seal off the ball by pinching the paper over the glued parts. Keep it as neat and tight as possible.

5. If you haven't already done so, cut your poppy petals out, with the stretch of the crepe paper going horizontally (from side to side) across the petal. Tease the paper apart by pulling gently to create a 3-D petal effect.

6. Glue the bottom of the petals to the now-covered polystyrene ball.

7. Repeat and glue all around the ball.

8. Your poppy should look like this.

9. Apply glue to the base, and then add the poppy to the other flowers on the wreath.

DRIED WREATHS

## Leaves

1. Cut out the green leaves and apply glue.

2. Place floristry wire down the middle of the leaf.

3. Get another leaf and pop it on top of the wire to cover it—apply more glue if necessary.

4. Stick the leaves directly into the wreath. Mold them slightly into a realistic shape.

**Tip:**
You can use tissue paper as an alternative to crepe paper, or why not try painting patterns with acrylic paint or felt-tip pens to make them look more realistic.

Do not get these paper flowers wet! Don't keep them too close to sources of flames (candles, fires, etc.), and avoid direct sunlight since this will fade their beautiful colors.

**To finish**
Continue to repeat these methods and attach flowers around the entire wreath.

WREATHS

# Feather Wreath

If you are blessed to live in the countryside, you can usually come by feathers quite easily. They are quite often kept as a by product on poultry farms—which is the most sustainable way to buy feathers. Otherwise, please do some research before buying from big online sites—their feathers could come from an unethical source. The concept of these feather wreaths is adaptable for a plethora of alternative materials—how about chopsticks or straws: anything straight, really! As long as you have a glue gun and a wreath base, you're good to go.

**Tools**
Glue gun
Scissors

**Materials**
Feathers
Reel wire
Straw wreath
Twine

## DRIED WREATHS

1

2
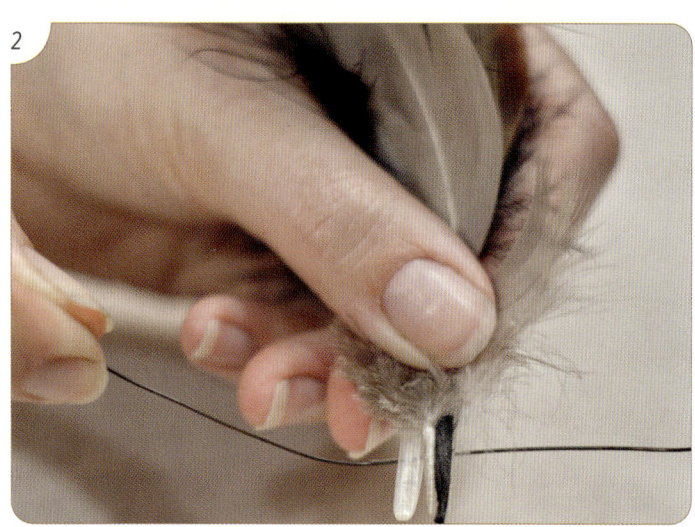

3

4

5

6a

# WREATHS

6b

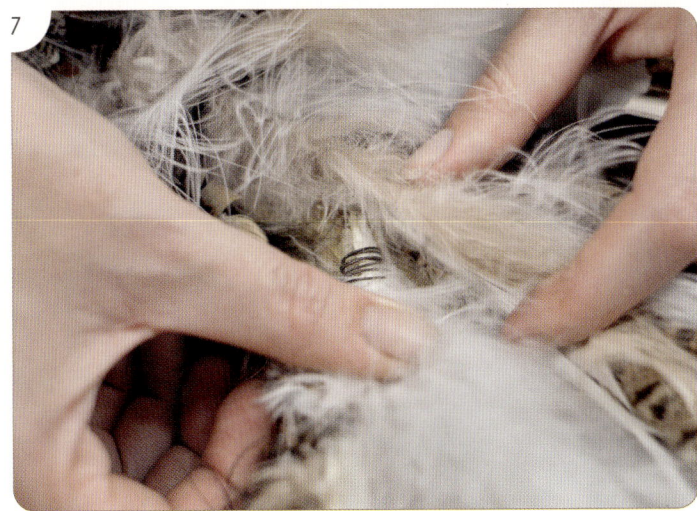

7

1. Create a simple hanging device, using the twine by wrapping it around the straw wreath, then cutting and tying it together.

2. This wreath is put together by creating miniature bunches of feathers. To do this, bunch together a few feathers that vary in color and texture, and using the reel wire, wrap them together at the stalk ends.

3. When all the feathers are tightly bound, cut the wire with some sharp scissors.

4. Continue making these small wraps of feathers, mixing up the colors, lengths, and textures for variety of shape and form.

5. With a heated-glue gun, apply glue to the base and all around the stalk ends of the feathers (especially on the underside).

6. Press the feathers firmly onto the wreath at the angle shown in the photos. Wait a few seconds for the hot glue to dry, then glue on the next bunch. Keep the bunches at the same angle of application all the way around the wreath.

7. Always work in the same direction—clockwise or counterclockwise—doesn't matter which, but stay consistent. Overlay each bunch over the last—you don't want to be "tucking" the feather bundles under each other; they should be laid on top, so you hide the stalk ends as you go around.

DRIED WREATHS

*8*

8. As you stick the bundles down, make sure all of the straw wreath base is covered. It is helpful to almost work from left to right while simultaneously working clockwise (or counterclockwise). This way you can use shorter bundles for the inner part of the wreath and the long ones at the outer.

   When you get back to the beginning, make sure you glue the last feathers down underneath the first ones, so you are not gluing on top of the feathers! Just lift the existing feathers up slightly and insert the bunch underneath.

**Tip:**
Collect feathers from ethical sources or weave in some raffia or chunky twine for a fuller, more boho look.

# Pine Cone Wreath

Pine cone wreaths are synonymous with fall and Christmas—jazz up your pine cones by spray-painting them or dipping them in PVA and glitter. These are everlasting—I think my mother still has one she made back in the 1980s! The joy is that they can be ever-evolving, something you can bring back for the kids to spruce up every year as a craft project. Don't be frightened to display it all year round; they're pretty timeless.

### Tools
Glue gun
Glue sticks
Scissors

### Materials
Acorn pods or seeds, + natural materials
Binding wire
Copper wire wreath (12 in./30 cm diameter)
Florists' wire
Foraged sticks or twigs
Mossing pins
Pine cones
Reindeer moss
Silver moss

DRIED WREATHS

1

2

3

4

5

6

# WREATHS

7

1. Place the materials and tools in front of you so you can see how the wreath can come together. Silver moss is generally very clumped, so tease it apart gently to make it easier to use. This also makes the materials go further.

2. Hold the silver moss on the wreath ring with your nondominant hand. With your dominant hand, hold the wreath wire on top of the moss and start wrapping it around the ring.

3. Carry on adding and wrapping the moss; don't add it all at once since it will fall off. Make sure you spread it out or the wreath will lack the surface area you need to attach the cones.

4. When you come to the end of the ring, cut the wire and poke it back into the moss to hide it. This doesn't need to be tied.

5. Wind florists' wire around the pine cones, near the base. If you don't have this wire, you could use lengths of binding wire instead.

6. Bend the wire to meet itself around the pine cone, as near the base as possible.

7. Twist the wire around itself so that you are able to hold the pine cone up simply by the wire. If it passes this test, it's good for the wreath.

## DRIED WREATHS

8. Repeat this process for every pine cone you have.

9. Cut the wire down so that it measures about 6 in. (15 cm) from the base of the pine cone to the end of the wire.

10. Holding the wreath in place, gently insert the wire into the moss. If you are worried about the wires scratching your door, then fold the ends of the wire back into the wreath, but be careful they don't poke out of the front!

11. Once you have placed the first few pine cones, you can start using your reindeer moss to decorate around them. Don't worry about completely covering your original silver moss base, since it looks lovely being exposed, but gently pin the reindeer moss into the base, using mossing pins.

12. Start chopping up any twigs you have, making sure to leave enough length to be poked into the base, while at the same time keeping it short so as not to protrude too much and cause an injury!

13. Insert the twigs between the pine cones, making everything look as natural as possible.

14. Using a glue gun, glue the backs of the acorn shells (or other natural foraged materials) in a decorative manner to the moss. If you're using damp, fresh moss, you may want to wait a few days until it has dried out to do this step.

DRIED WREATHS

15

15. Consider the overall balance of the design when fixing the glued pieces in place. Make sure you spread your material evenly over the whole wreath, to get a fully rounded effect.

    Once completed, you can make a hanger out of any suitable colored ribbon or wire, and attach it to the original copper wreath base.

**Tip:**
Use different sizes and types of pine cones. Also, nuts and seeds add interest with their different shapes and colors. You can always add some lights, glitter, or spray-paint the whole wreath for a uniform look—or be daring and do everything!

# Rag Wreath

This wreath is a fantastic way of using up any old clothes that are too far gone for the thrift store, or children's clothes that you can't get persistent stains out of! Although time-consuming, the overall effect—that of a rag rug—is amazing at the end. I would suggest picking a color scheme and keeping to it—we have used shades of teal and black. Different textures are also very welcome here for contrast and interest.

## Tools
Fabric scissors

## Materials
Copper wreath ring
Mixture of scrap materials
Ribbon
Twine

DRIED WREATHS

1

2

3

4

5

6

WREATHS

7

8

1. Set out all of your materials and tools in front of you. Sort the materials into attractive color groupings. Then, start by tying the end of the twine to the copper wreath.

2. Without cutting the twine, wind it tightly around the ring.

3. When you get back to the beginning, cut the twine and tie it off.

4. Begin chopping up your scrap material to approximately 1 in. (2 cm) wide and 6 in. (15 cm) long.

5. Tie the rag to the wreath, using just one simple knot (you may want to double-knot some of the slippery satin-type materials).

6. Work your way around the outside of the wreath, tying material strips next to each other without spaces.

7. When tying the material to the ring, make sure to mix up the colors and textures, and try not to get too many of the same next to each other.

8. Once the outer edge has been completed, do the inner edge. Alternatively, you can work on both at the same time as you move your way around.

# DRIED WREATHS

9. Once the inner and outer sides are done, you will be able to see any gaps that need filling.

10. You can fill these gaps by tying pieces of material to the twine and slipping it up and down and into place.

11. Find or cut a longer ribbon, and tie it into a hanger for the door.

**Tip:**
Switch up you color palette—simplify the scheme by sticking to just one hue, or go crazy and make a rainbow-inspired rag wreath!

# Occasion Wreaths

# Christmas Bauble Wreath

I almost prefer these to traditional Christmas wreaths, and they are a great way to use up all the baubles that have been rendered surplus to the Christmas tree. I would definitely choose a color scheme and stick to it—too many conflicting colors can make the wreath look a bit trashy. This is a brilliant thing to make with the kids—get them to decorate their own bauble and you can swap, replace, or add new ones each year.

## Tools
Glue
Glue gun

## Materials
Baubles
Polystyrene wreath base
Ribbon

OCCASION WREATHS

1
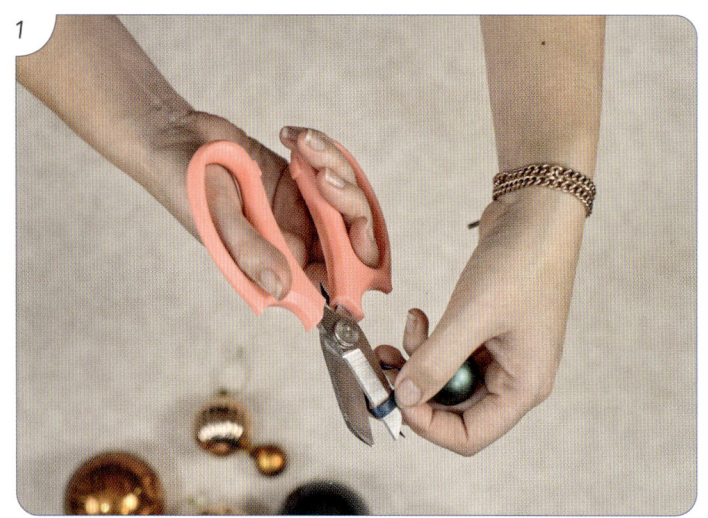

2

3

4

5

6

# WREATHS

7

1. Start off by cutting the hanging ribbons or wires from your baubles.

2. After heating up the glue gun, choose your largest baubles. Liberally apply glue to the top of each bauble—this will be your attaching point.

3. Start with the inner ring—glue the bauble ends and stick them to the inner edge of the polystyrene wreath. Angle their tops down so the hanging end is not visible when looking from above.

4. Once done, work on the outer edge of the wreath. Again, choose the biggest baubles you have. Mix them up by not placing the same ones next to each other—choose different colors and textures.

5. Complete the outer ring; if there are any gaps, then that will be where you start when you do the inner section.

6. For the inner wreath, again start with the largest baubles.

7. Try to place them so they aren't built up too high, but rather as one varied layer around the ring.

OCCASION WREATHS

8. When you have used all your baubles up, you'll see which gaps still need filling.

9. Apply small- and medium-sized baubles in the same manner as you glued on the large ones—work from the top of the wreath down.

10. A large variety of sizes, as well as different-colored and textured baubles, is beneficial for the overall design and makes the entire wreath sing!

Ta-da! You can glue a piece of ribbon to the polystyrene at the back to make a colorful hanger.

**Tip:**
Add bells, LED lights, ribbons, or even a few sprigs of fresh festive foliage and berries. And why not finish with a huge decorative bow?

# Pop-Pom Wreath

Although they've been included in the materials list, the pom-pom makers aren't an essential bit of kit—there are plenty of online tutorials that will show you how to make pom-poms from a simple bit of cardboard. I love making this wreath. Even though the pom-poms are fairly labor intensive, the assembly of the wreath itself is very quick and very effective. Try some glittery wools for Christmas or muted colors for an Easter theme.

### Tools
Glue gun
Glue tubes
Fabric scissors

### Materials
Mixed yarn/wool colors
Polystyrene wreath ring
Pom-pom makers
Snips

## OCCASION WREATHS

1

2

3
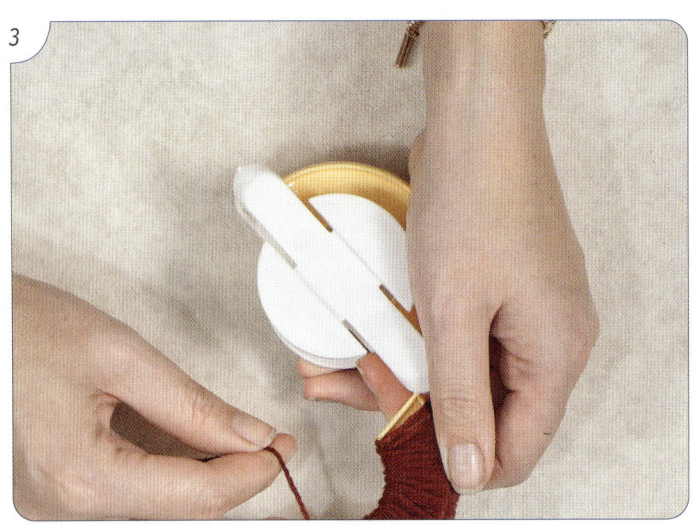

4
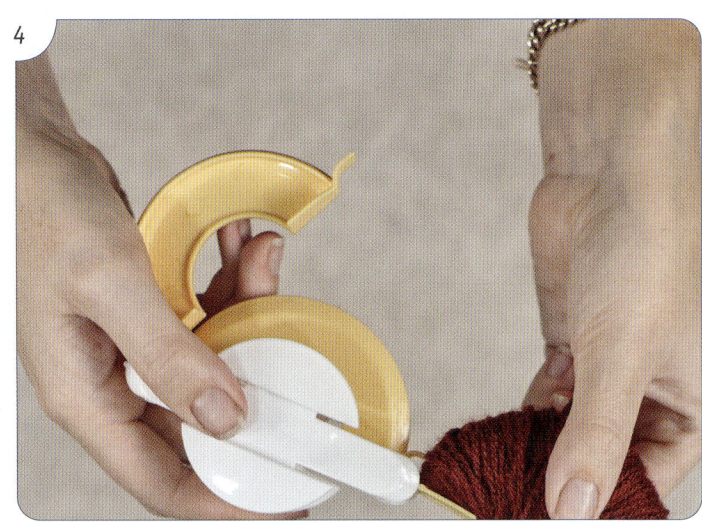

5

6

WREATHS

1. Open up the largest pom-pom maker by pulling one of the sides out. We've used a plastic one here, but you can always make your own from cardboard (see page 11).

2. Start a piece of yarn on one of the edges—hold it in place (no need to tie a knot in it).

3. Wrap the yarn from one side to the other, over and over again, to create a thick band of yarn.

4. Keep wrapping the yarn around the edges until the yarn "fills up" the middle segment—the whole side should look like a bulging semicircle.

5. Close the side of the pom-pom maker. Cut the yarn end.

6. After repeating the same process on the other side, use the snips to cut along the edge of the pom-pom maker (the sharper the scissors/snips, the easier it is to cut).

7. When the pom-pom maker is opened, the yarn will fluff out: keep holding it firmly so the individual bits don't fall out.

8. Cut a long piece of yarn from the original ball—use the same color if possible.

9. Pull the piece of yarn around the pom-pom maker and tie it tightly.

OCCASION WREATHS

10

13

11

14a

12

14b
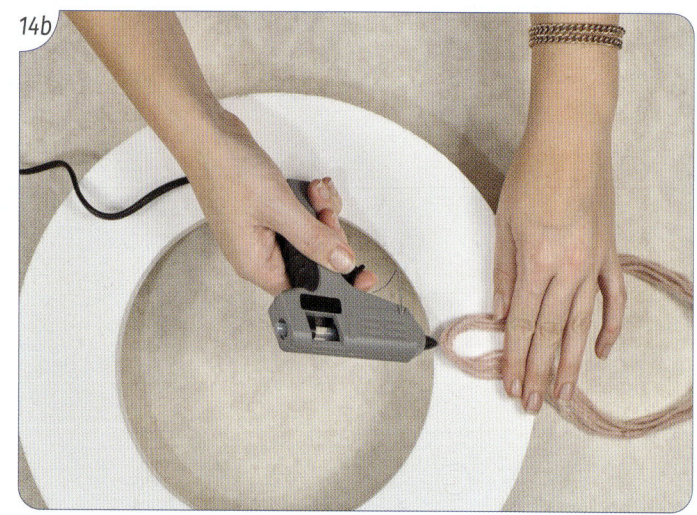

WREATHS

10. Open the pom-pom maker and carefully remove it from the yarn ball.

11. Fluff up the pom-pom.

12. Trim off any loose or ragged threads.

13. Take some time to ensure all the ends are trimmed down and you get a nice rounded pom-pom. Repeat this process for all the other colored pom-poms you want to make. Vary the sizes you make for variety.

14. Wrap yarn around on itself and make a hook for the pom-pom wreath before gluing on the pom-poms.

15. After your glue gun has heated up, liberally apply a large glob to the side of your first pom-pom (make it a big one). Stick it firmly to the polystyrene wreath.

16. Repeat this process, making sure you use different colors and sizes of pom-pom as you go around, filling in all the gaps.

17. Carry on around the wreath, making sure all the colors are evenly spread and none of the underlying wreath ring is visible.

**Tip:**
Use different colors and mixed kinds of yarn—metallic, wool, thread, cotton, chunky—whatever you can find. How about creating an ombré effect by starting with one color and blending into another until you get back to the start? Or make a color wheel. Use your creativity!

WREATHS

# Felt Flower Wreath

Kids will love to help make this wreath, since it takes skill to draw around the template and cut a lot of the same pieces up! Because of the nature of the materials, they look fabulous on children's bedroom doors or as gifts for unsuspecting grandparents. If you don't already have one, invest in a glue gun for this project—you can get them in craft stores for a few dollars, and you won't regret it. While you're there, buy some felt as well.

### Tools
Glue gun
Glue sticks
Sharp scissors
Templates

### Materials
Ball of yarn
Copper wreath 12 in. (30 cm) diameter
Felt — multicolored sheets in your theme colors
Fiberfill stuffing
Miniature pom-poms

OCCASION WREATHS

WREATHS

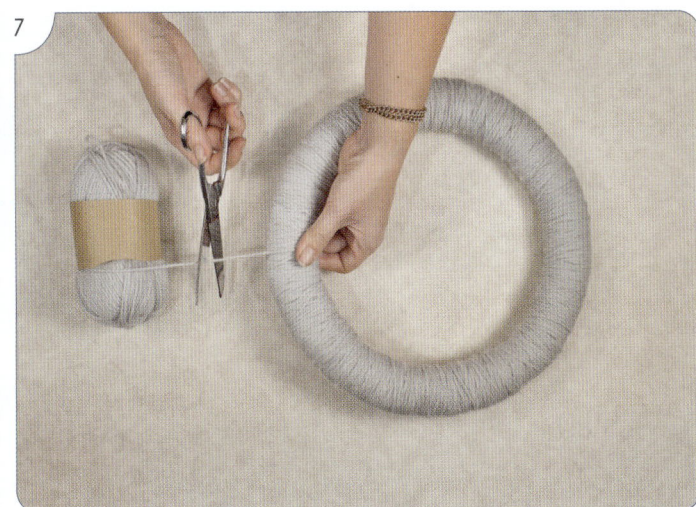

1. Bunch some of the fiberfill stuffing (or whatever kind of stuffing you're using) on top of one section of the copper wreath ring.

2. Tie off the wool end of your yarn ball to a section of the copper ring.

3. Start to wrap your wool around the stuffing. Don't pull it too tightly or the stuffing will lose its shape, but also don't leave it too loose, so the stuffing can work its way out.

4. Attach tennis-ball-sized wads of stuffing one ball at a time, as you wind the wool around the wreath. Pull and mold the shaping as you work.

5. Continue shaping and winding all the way around the wreath in the same manner.

6. Don't cut the yarn—carry on wrapping it around the wadding to form a solid layer of wool.

7. Once you have gotten back to the beginning, cut the wool and tie it off to another piece of wool on the wreath.

Trace or scan the templates on page 127. There are eleven different flower and foliage elements on this wreath, and instructions for each of them are on the following pages. It is a good idea to make one of each type and lay them out on the wreath base to give you a rough idea of how many you think you would like to have of each one. This way you can vary the colors and number and type of each element to your own style.

OCCASION WREATHS

# WREATHS

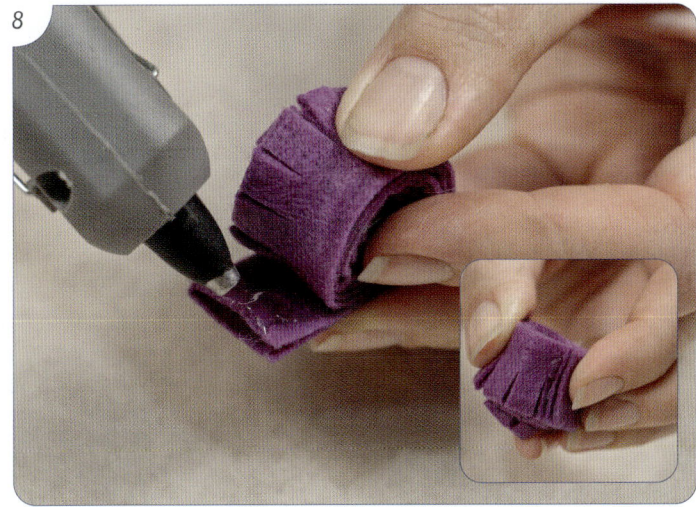

## F1

1. Cut out six pieces each, using templates F1a and F1b, and seven using template F1c. Glue the six F1a pieces one on top of the other to form the first layer of the flower.

2. Continue to glue, using the six F1b pieces and five of the F1c pieces. Stagger the leaves to create a succulent shape.

3. Place a bit of hot glue at the bottom middle of the remaining two F1c pieces. While the glue is still hot, use your forefinger and thumb to fold the leaf.

4. Glue the rolled pieces into the center to create a 3-D silhouette.

**Please note:** the leaves on the wreath (**F3**) are made using the F1a template and step 3 above.

## F2

5. Cut out template F2 and glue along one of the edges. Fold the felt in half and glue it to itself.

6. Feather-cut the folded side, make the cuts about half the width of the piece. Make the incisions about 1/3 in. (10 mm) apart.

7. Put a glue glob on one end of the felt. Roll the cut-out over the glue glob.

8. Pop another glue glob at the other end and roll over it. Press it down to let the glue set.

## OCCASION WREATHS

1

2

3

4a

4b

5

# WREATHS

## F5

1. Cut out one piece each, using templates F5a, F5b, and F5c. With the glue gun, attach them all together by putting blobs of glue in between the layers and stacking them one on top of the other.

2. Attach a miniature pom-pom to the center of the top piece—hot-glue and press down on the felt.

**Please note:** Flower **F8** is made in the same way. In this case, enlarging the templates for the three layers of petals and using an F2 flower instead of a pom-pom in the center.

**F10** also uses a similar method. In this case, cut out two pieces each, using templates F10a, F10b, and F10c. Then stack them, gluing as you go, one on top of the other. Start with the largest (F10a) at the bottom and rotate each layer.

## F6

3. Cut out the daisy design template (F6). Apply hot glue to one of the miniature pom-poms. Attach the pom-pom to the middle of the flower.

**Please note:** Flower **F4** is made in exactly the same way, just using a different color for the felt and a larger miniature pom-pom.

## F7

4. Cut out around 10 of the same-sized long triangular-shaped leaves (template F7). Apply glue to the large ends of the triangles and begin to attach them to a small pompom.

5. Continue to apply glue around the pom-pom and cover the end of it.

6. Once the outer is covered, fill the inner with more leaves.

OCCASION WREATHS

# WREATHS

5a

5b

### F9
1. Cut out the piece from template F9, as shown in the picture.

### F11
2. To make F11, use templates F1a and F1b, cutting out a few of each. Stack and stagger the leaves on top of one another, working from largest to smallest. Glue in between. Continue to glue, staggering the leaves to create a succulent shape.

3. Fold the last 2 smallest leaves in half and glue in the center of the fold to hold them in place.

4. Glue to the center of the succulent to create a 3-D silhouette.

### Assembly
5. Once you have decided how many elements you want and have finished creating them, begin to glue them to the wreath base. Here they are grouped by color, but you can apply them in any order you wish.

OCCASION WREATHS

**Assembly, continued**

6. Attach the flowers by layering them on top of each other.

7. After all the other elements are glued down, you can add any extra leaves (**F3**, see page 105) to fill in gaps or just for balance.

Attach the wreath to the door in any way you want—by adding a piece of string and some glue, or a simple S hook.

**Tip:**
Try designing stylized versions of your favorite types of flower or succulent. Use different colors. You can also finish the wreath off by wrapping LED string lights around it.

# Easter Egg Wreath

We've used a lot of faux eggs in this wreath, but if you have the time and the patience, you could blow your own eggs and paint them yourself. (Just be warned—you'll have to eat a lot of meringue and drink a lot of whiskey sours to use up all of those eggs!) The joy of painting the eggs yourself is that you can again choose any color scheme that fits your house, or just leave them au naturel—just try to get a few different sizes and varieties.

### Tools
Glue gun
Glue sticks
Scissors

### Materials
Egg shells
Foraged sticks/twigs
Mixture of faux eggs
Natural-colored ribbons
Natural wreath
Small feathers
Twigs

## OCCASION WREATHS

1

2

3

4

5

6

WREATHS

7

1. Start by inserting the feathers in random places around the natural wreath; do quite a considerable amount. If they aren't staying put by just poking them into the wreath, then use a glue gun to affix them.

2. When this is done, choose the largest of your faux eggs and drop a good blob of glue on the base (or whichever bit you don't want to see).

3. Once the glue is in place, apply the egg to the wreath and hold it in place until it's set.

4. Repeat this exercise with all the big eggs, then all the smaller eggs. Glue a mixture of different eggs near each other in clusters, since the different colors and textures will complement each other.

5. Use more smaller eggs than large ones, to give the impression that the wreath is really full.

6. Chop down any of the twigs that are too long: you don't want them to catch on people as they go past.

7. Carefully poke the twigs in between the existing eggs. Apply glue on top to keep them in place.

OCCASION WREATHS

8. Once the eggs and twigs are securely in place, you can start gluing the reindeer moss into the gaps to pad out the filling.

9. Position the broken eggshells into any other gaps with big blobs of glue.

10. Using two different color ribbons, tie them around the entire wreath to use as a hanger.

**Tip:**
Make the wreath with real hand-blown eggs. Leave them natural or paint and decorate them—this is a fun project all of its own. You could weave in some fresh spring flowers too, for a special occasion.

# Halloween Wreath

I wanted to make an alternative wreath just to show that not all wreaths need to be round! I personally love the textures of this wreath—matte black paint makes so many things look modern. You can pick up any kind of seasonal décor in thrift stores, so it really is a budget wreath. You can use exactly the same method to make different-shaped wreaths—hearts and stars are popular—for different occasions!

### Tools
Glue gun
Glue sticks
Scissors

### Materials
Black matte spray
Black ribbon
Copper wreath ring
Natural wreath
Pliers (that can cut wire)
Reel wire
Spooky decorations — plastic spiders, snakes, etc.
Synthetic cobwebs

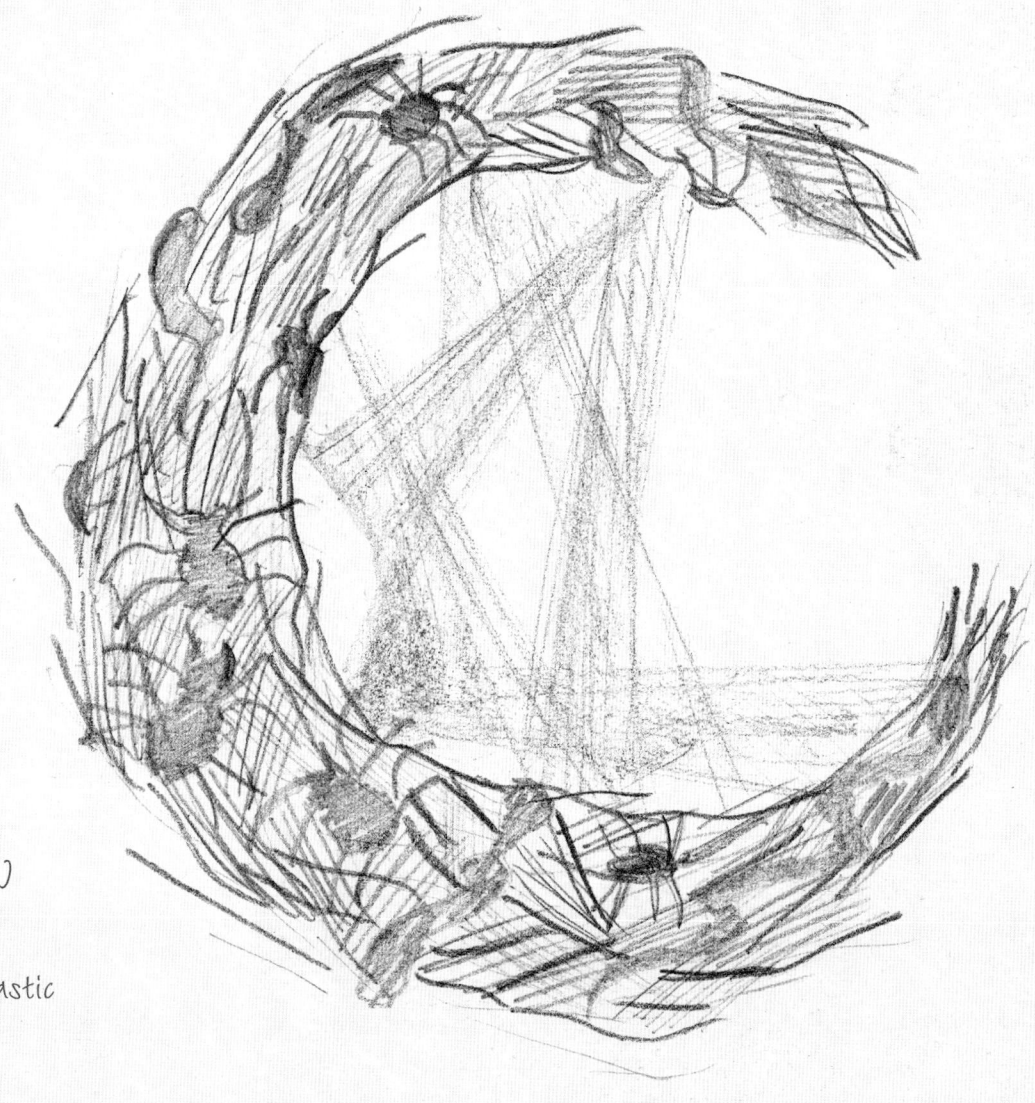

## OCCASION WREATHS

1
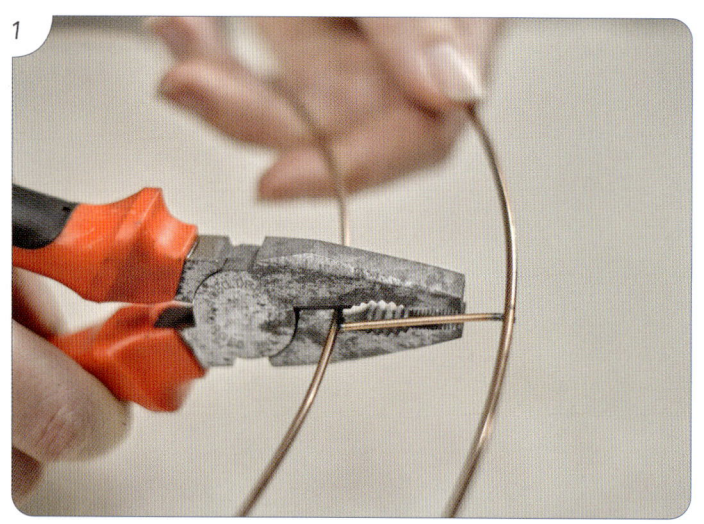

3b

2
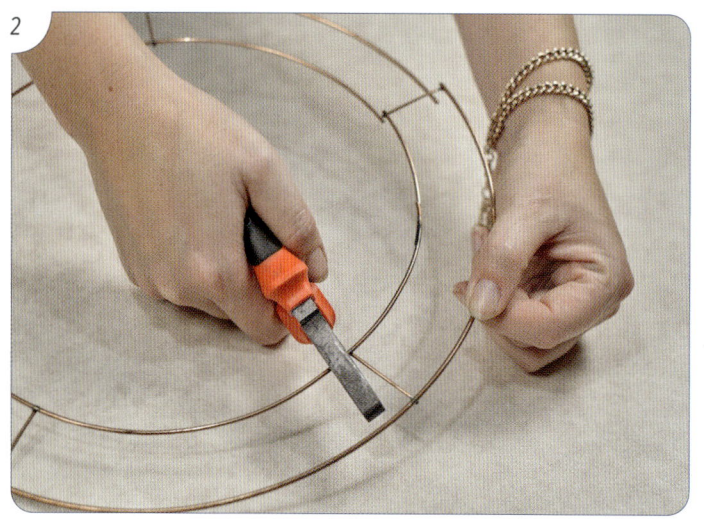

4

3a

5a

# WREATHS

1. With pliers, cut the copper wreath next to a joint.

2. Use the pliers again to cut off the rest of an entire section of the wreath to make a crescent shape.

3. Using the reel wire, bind together the two wire edges. Wind the wire tightly around the ends so that they won't come loose. Cut the reel wire.

4. Repeat on the opposite side—you should be forming a crescent shape.

5. Now to work with the natural wreath: cut the twine binding it together. Loosen and unfold the wreath.

6. Chop the wreath in half and then double it up on itself—so that you have a lot of twigs in a sort of semi-circle.

7. Start binding the twigs to the copper crescent shape. Bind it to only one side of the wreath (so the copper crescent is the underside). You're going to work upward from this base.

OCCASION WREATHS

8

10b

9

11

10a

12

# WREATHS

13

8. When you have bound all the twigs to the copper base, cut the binding wire and wrap the end around it.

9. Using scissors, neaten the edges of your crescent moon by chopping off any stray twigs.

10. With a glue gun, liberally coat the underside of your creepy spiders, insects, and other spooky decorations. Firmly place them on the wreath and hold them until the glue sets (about 10 seconds or so). Repeat attaching creatures all over the wreath—as many as you desire.

11. Once it's all glued down, go outside and spray the entire wreath with a can of matte black spray paint. Goggles and masks are advised here.

12. When the wreath is thoroughly dry, tease the faux cobweb apart and hook it onto stray twigs across the back of the crescent. Use lots, to make the cobweb really obvious (it can disappear otherwise).

13. Spread the cobweb across the wreath from side to side to create a web effect.

OCCASION WREATHS

14. Hook or glue a spider into the middle of the web.

15. To hang the Halloween wreath from your door, tie the black ribbon around the top edge of the crescent. Are you really sure that you added enough spiders?

---

**Tip:**
Alternatively, make a full wreath instead of a crescent, then add bats or spooky eyes! You could even make a basic star by using twigs or sticks and create a spider web by weaving around some white string. Add some black glitter too!

---

# Paper Wreath Templates

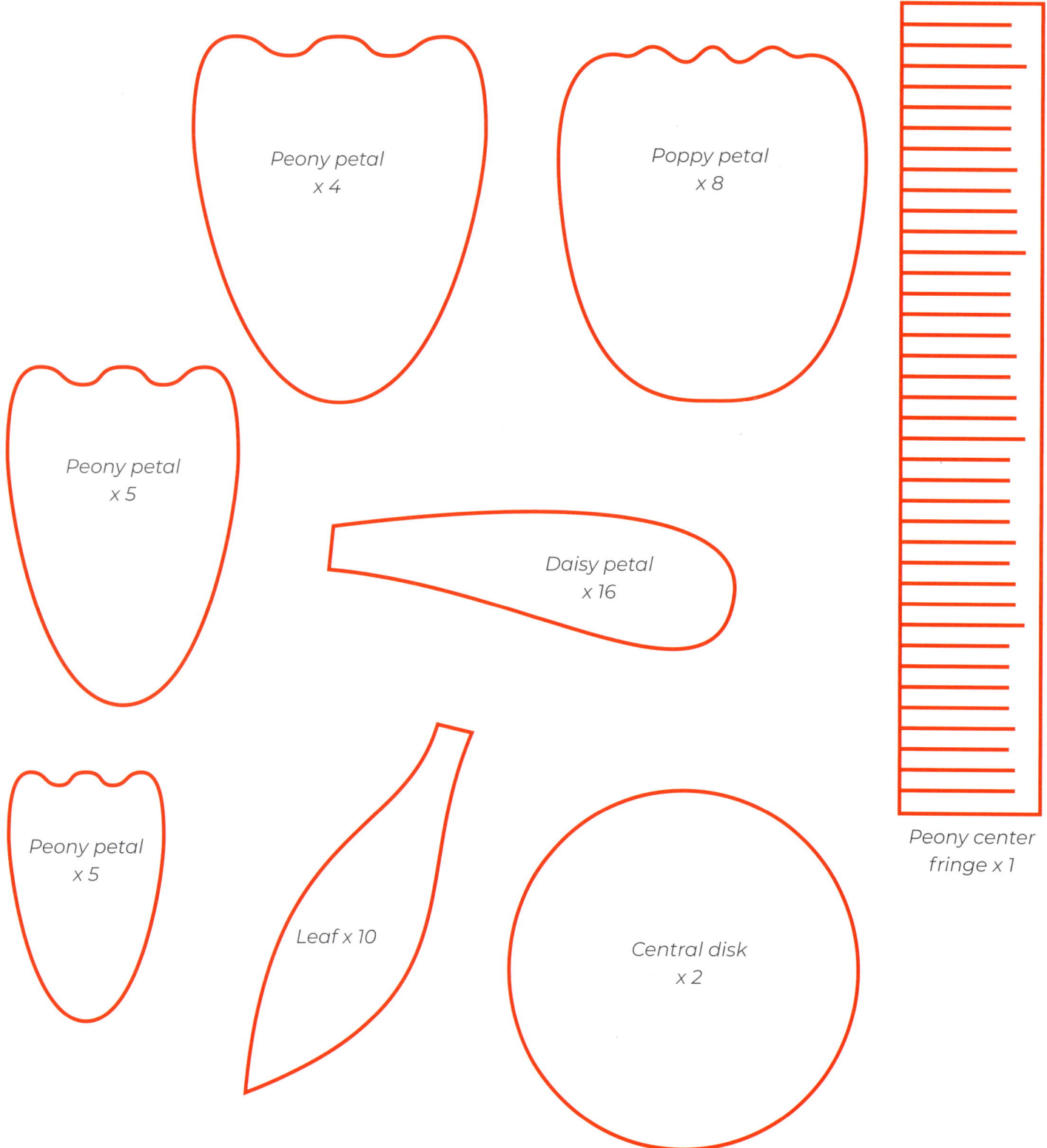

Alys Dobbie started off life as an antique dealer and restorer and has transferred her skills in French polishing and marquetry to creating amazing wreaths and terrariums.

This career change saw her retraining as a florist at a local agricultural college, and, seeing how very "traditional" all the wreath making was, she decided to experiment with different materials to create some beautiful enchanted circles.

Alys now runs workshops from her houseplant shop "Between Two Thorns" in Brighton, UK. The most popular workshop she runs is her succulent wreath workshop. The very nature and beauty of a succulent wreath is that it is totally organic, a living wreath that will change season by season.

www.betweentwothorns.com